Discover! 6

Oxford Read and Discover

Your Amazing Body

Robert Quin

T0055639

Contents

OXFORD
UNIVERSITY PRESS

OXFORD
UNIVERSITY PRESS

Great Clarendon Street, Oxford OX2 6DP

Oxford University Press is a department of the University of Oxford. It furthers the University's objective of excellence in research, scholarship, and education by publishing worldwide in

Oxford New York

Auckland Cape Town Dar es Salaam Hong Kong Karachi Kuala Lumpur Madrid Melbourne Mexico City Nairobi New Delhi Shanghai Taipei Toronto

With offices in

Argentina Austria Brazil Chile Czech Republic France Greece Guatemala Hungary Italy Japan Poland Portugal Singapore South Korea Switzerland Thailand Turkey Ukraine Vietnam

OXFORD and OXFORD ENGLISH are registered trade marks of Oxford University Press in the UK and in certain other countries

ISBN: 978 0 19 464558 4

An Audio Pack containing this book and an Audio download is also available ISBN: 978 0 19 402253 8

This book is also available as an e-Book, ISBN: 978 0 19 410916 1

An accompanying Activity Book is also available ISBN: 978 0 19 464568 3

Printed in China

This book is printed on paper from certified and well-managed sources.

ACKNOWLEDGEMENTS

Illustrations by: Kelly Kennedy pp.6, 11, 22, 25; Ian Moores pp.6 (babies), 9, 13, 16, 17, 21, 22 (heart), 23 (kidneys), 25 (digestion), 26, 30, 38, 42, 44, 46.

The Publishers would also like to thank the following for their kind permission to reproduce photographs and other copyright material: Alamy pp.32 (© tbkmedia.de), 35 (Peter Newton); Corbis pp.19 (© P Deliss/Godong/inhaler); Getty Images p.18 (Johner/Johner Images/scuba diver); Oxford University Press p.3, 5 (muscle cells), 7, 8, 10, 11, 12, 14, 19 (no smoking sign), 40; Photolibrary pp.4 (Garry DeLong), 18 (Peter Giovannini/imagebroker.net/climber), 31 (Pawel Liera/Britain on View); Science Photo Library p.5 (SCIMAT/blood cells, Steve Gschmeissner/nerve cells), 15, 20 (Science Source), 23 (AJ Photo/Hop Americain), 24 (Maximilian Stock Ltd), 27 (Jim Varney), 28 (Francois Paquet-Durand), 29 (Pasieka), 33 (Jim Selby), 34 (Steve Gschmeissner), 49 (Pasieka).

With thanks to Ann Fullick for science checking

Introduction

Your body is amazing! It lets you move around, discover the world, and communicate with other people. Your body is made of millions of tiny cells that work together in different ways. All these cells need air, water, and other nutrients to grow, to reproduce, and to stay healthy.

What parts of the body do you see below?
What do these parts of the body do?
Do you know how they work?

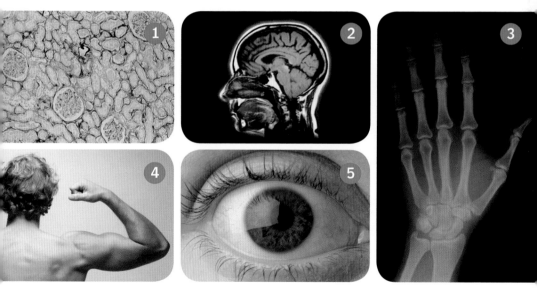

Now read and discover more about your amazing body!

1 Cells and Growth

Cells are the smallest living parts of all plants and animals. The tiniest living things have only one cell. Other living things have many cells. Do you know how many cells a human body has? More than ten trillion! Isn't that incredible?

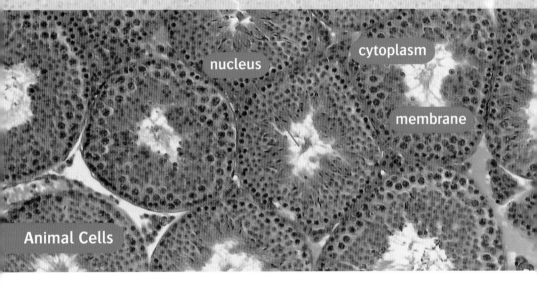

nucleus

cytoplasm

membrane

Animal Cells

Inside Your Cells

Each cell in your body has many parts. Inside the cell there's a jelly called cytoplasm. Most human cells also have a nucleus. The nucleus controls everything that happens in the cell. The outside layer of the cell is called the membrane. It protects the cell and keeps the cytoplasm inside. Some things, like water, can go through tiny holes in the membrane.

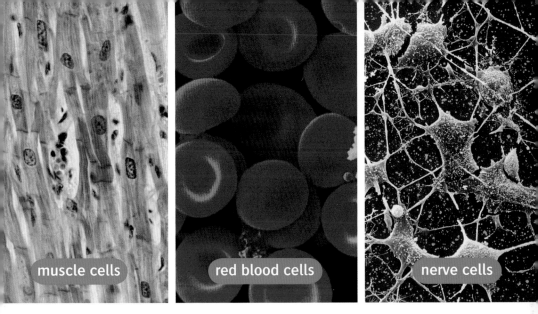

muscle cells

red blood cells

nerve cells

Different Cells

Your cells use nutrients from your food to grow. They also work to keep your body strong and healthy. They are like tiny factories! Different types of cell are different shapes. Your muscle cells are long and thin, your red blood cells are round, and your nerve cells are more irregular shapes.

Cell Reproduction

Most of your body's cells can reproduce themselves. Each cell divides to make two new cells. This lets your body grow and change. This is also how your body replaces cells that are old or damaged.

Discover!

Your body produces more than two million red blood cells every second! Each cell only lives for about 120 days.

The First Nine Months

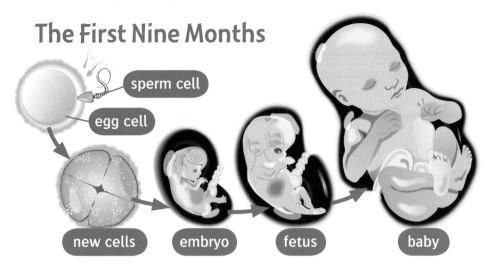

sperm cell

egg cell

new cells   embryo   fetus   baby

Human babies grow from two tiny cells that are produced by their parents. The mother produces an egg cell, and the father produces a sperm cell. These two cells join to create one new cell. Then the new cell divides to make many cells that form an embryo. When the embryo gets bigger it's called a fetus. After nine months of growth, the baby is finally born.

Childhood

Children grow very quickly in their first years of life. They get bigger, and their arms and legs get much longer. Children usually learn to walk and talk in their first two years. When they are older, they become more independent, and they learn to care for themselves.

Discover! On their first birthday, most babies weigh three times more than when they were born!

Adolescence

Between the ages of 11 and 15, children become adolescents. They get taller, and their bodies change as they grow into young adults. For most people, these changes continue until they are about 20 years old. After that, most people don't get taller, but they can get bigger and fatter.

Adulthood and Old Age

Adults continue to change as they get older. They can also have children and start new families. Older people often get lines and wrinkles on their skin. Their hair can also turn gray or white. Many older people stop working. Then they can spend more time with their family and friends.

Different Times of Life

→ Go to pages 36–37 for activities.

Skin, Hair, and Nails

Your skin covers the outside of your body. Hair grows from your skin, and you have fingernails and toenails. These parts of your body help to protect you. Do you know how?

Your Skin

Your skin protects the inside of your body from dirt and germs. Skin is also elastic, so you can move your body easily. When you get older, your skin becomes less elastic. That's why people get wrinkles! Your skin protects you from heat and cold, too. It helps to keep your body at the right temperature.

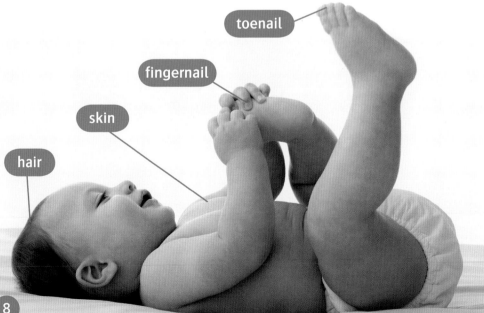

toenail

fingernail

skin

hair

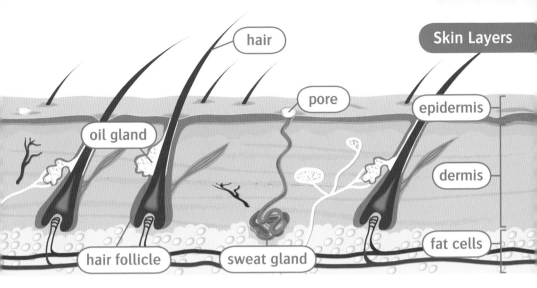

hair

pore

epidermis

oil gland

dermis

fat cells

hair follicle

sweat gland

The inside layer of your skin is called the dermis. It has thin tubes called follicles, where hair grows. Next to the follicles, there are tiny oil glands that produce oil. This oil keeps your skin soft and waterproof. The dermis also has lots of sweat glands. They produce sweat when you get too hot. Under the dermis, there are fat cells. They keep you warm when it's cold.

The epidermis is the outside layer of your skin. The cells on the surface of your skin are dead, but there are always lots of new cells growing under them. Your epidermis also has lots of tiny holes called pores. This is where sweat comes out. When the sweat dries, it helps to cool your body.

Discover!

Your skin contains a chemical called melanin. Dark skin has more melanin than light skin. Melanin helps to protect your skin from the sun, but don't forget to wear suncream!

Your Hair

Your hair isn't made of living cells. It's made of a special protein called keratin. Your hair also contains melanin, just like your skin. Dark hair contains more melanin than red hair or fair hair.

Hair is important because it helps to keep you warm. You have more hair on your head because that's where you lose the most heat. When you feel cold, the hairs on the rest of your body stand up. This keeps warm air near your skin.

Discover!

You have about 100,000 hairs on your head. You lose about 100 hairs every day, but then new hairs replace them.

Your Nails

Your nails are made of keratin, like your hair, but they are much harder. Your nails are important because they protect the soft ends of your fingers and toes. You can also use your nails to pick up small things.

Each nail grows from a root, and the pink part under the nail is called the nail bed. Your fingernails grow about 2 or 3 millimeters every month, so you need to cut them often. Your toenails only grow about 1 millimeter every month.

Discover!

If you hurt one of your fingernails it can fall off, but then it will grow back again. It usually takes from three to six months to grow a new fingernail.

→ Go to pages 38–39 for activities.

Bones and Muscles

Your bones fit together to make a skeleton that supports your body. Your muscles let you move around and do things. Do you know how your bones and muscles work together?

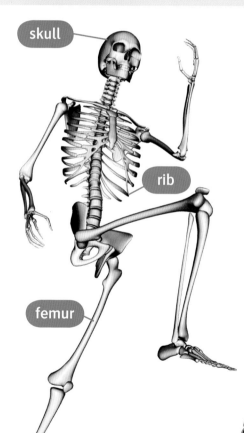

skull

rib

femur

A Model of a Skeleton

Your Skeleton

Your skeleton has 206 different bones. The largest bone in your body is the femur in the top of your leg. Your smallest bones are the ossicles. They are three tiny bones in each of your ears. Some bones help to protect the soft parts inside your body. For example, your ribs protect your heart and lungs, and the bones in your skull protect your brain.

Discover!

Each of your hands has 27 bones, and each of your feet has 26.

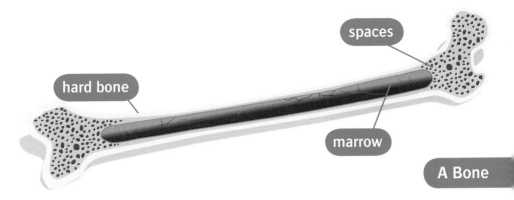

spaces

hard bone

marrow

A Bone

Inside Your Bones

Some bones, like the ones in your skull, are solid. Other bones, like the femur, are hard on the outside and have lots of tiny spaces inside. This makes them lighter and easier to move. Large bones also have a soft, red part in the center, called marrow. This is where your body grows new red blood cells.

Joints are places where bones meet and move together. Different joints work in different ways. For example, your hip can move in lots of ways, but your knee bends only one way. Inside each joint, there is flexible cartilage. It stops the ends of the bones touching. That would hurt!

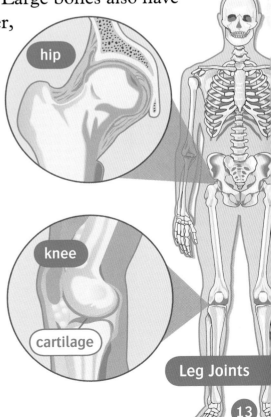

hip

knee

cartilage

Leg Joints

13

Your Muscles

A muscle is made of millions of long cells. When these cells contract, they pull together. This makes the muscle shorter. When the cells relax, the muscle can get longer again, but another muscle needs to pull on it. That's why your muscles always work together in pairs. For example, when the bicep muscle in your arm contracts, it pulls on your tricep muscle. Your tricep muscle relaxes and becomes longer.

You can contract and relax your voluntary muscles whenever you want. For example, you can use your arm muscles to lift things. Voluntary muscles are joined to your bones by strong fibers called tendons. When the muscles contract, they pull on the tendons and move the bones.

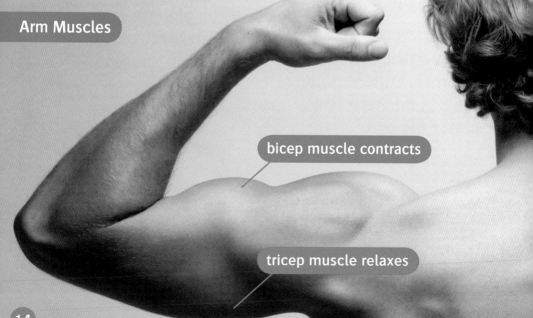

Arm Muscles

bicep muscle contracts

tricep muscle relaxes

Some of your muscles work automatically. You don't need to think about controlling them. These are involuntary muscles. Your heart is a good example. It never stops pumping blood. There are involuntary muscles in your stomach, too. When you eat, these muscles contract and relax to mix your food.

A Heart

Your heart beats about 100,000 times every day. That's more than 36,500,000 times every year!

Protein and Calcium

To grow muscles and to keep them strong, you need to eat food that has lots of protein. You can get protein from food like meat, fish, eggs, beans, and milk. You also need calcium for strong bones and teeth. You can get calcium from milk and dairy products. Some vegetables, like spinach, also have lots of calcium.

Go to pages 40–41 for activities.

Lungs and Breathing

All living things need oxygen. Some animals, like fish, take oxygen from water. Other animals take oxygen from the air that they breathe. You get oxygen this way, too!

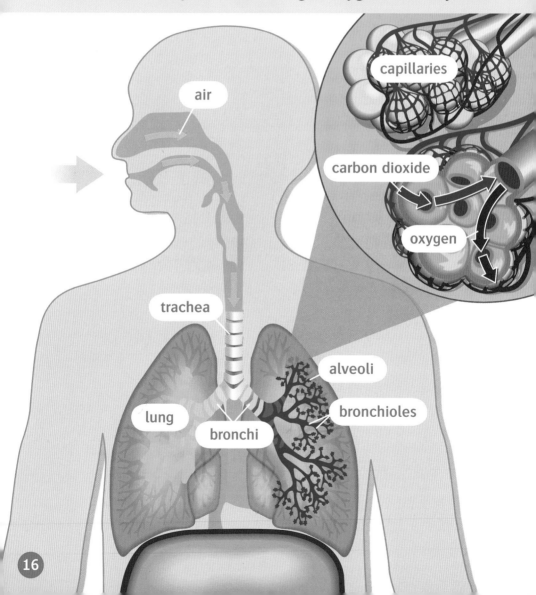

capillaries

air

carbon dioxide

oxygen

trachea

alveoli

lung

bronchioles

bronchi

Breathing In

When you breathe in, the air goes in through your nose or your mouth. Then it goes down into your chest through a large tube called the trachea. In your chest, the trachea divides into two smaller tubes called bronchi – one goes to your right lung, and the other goes to your left lung. In your lungs, the bronchi divide into smaller tubes called bronchioles. At the end of the bronchioles there are tiny air bags called alveoli. The oxygen that you breathe goes here.

In Your Lungs

Around the alveoli there are lots of tiny tubes that transport blood. They are called capillaries. The walls of the capillaries are very thin, so oxygen from your alveoli can go through them into your blood. Then your red blood cells take the oxygen to all the other cells in your body.

Breathing Out

Your cells use oxygen, but they also produce a waste gas called carbon dioxide. Your blood takes this gas to your lungs. Then the gas goes through the capillaries and into your alveoli. The carbon dioxide leaves your body when you breathe out.

Discover!

Your alveoli are very tiny. You have about 250 million of them in each of your lungs!

air tank

mouthpiece

Underwater

Fish can take the oxygen that they need from water, but people can't! Most people can only hold their breath for a minute or two. Then they need to breathe air again. Some divers can stay underwater for a longer time because they use an air tank. They breathe air from the tank through a special mouthpiece.

mask

At High Altitudes

When people climb high mountains, in places like the Himalayas, it's difficult to breathe. The air at high altitudes is thinner, so there is less oxygen. To get enough oxygen, mountain climbers need to breathe faster. Some climbers take oxygen tanks and breathe the oxygen through a mask.

Asthma

Some people have asthma. Their lungs get irritated very easily. When this happens, their bronchioles contract and get very small. This makes breathing more difficult. People with asthma can use an inhaler to take medicine. It lets them breathe the medicine into their lungs. This relaxes their bronchioles, so that they can breathe more easily again.

Using an Inhaler

Don't Smoke!

Smoking is very bad for your body, and especially for your lungs. When people smoke, it makes their lungs very dirty, so they can't breathe well. Smoking also causes many other health problems, like lung cancer and heart disease. Care for your lungs, and don't smoke!

Discover! The World Health Organization says that smoking kills about five million people every year.

→ Go to pages 42–43 for activities.

5 Blood and Circulation

Your blood takes oxygen and other nutrients to all the cells in your body. It also takes away waste from your cells. The muscles in your heart pump the blood to keep it moving all the time.

Your Blood

In your blood, you have millions of tiny red blood cells. They get oxygen from your lungs and then they take it to the rest of your body. You also have many white blood cells. They help to protect you from diseases. Your body produces more white blood cells when you are sick or when you have an infection. Your blood also contains nutrients like sugar, proteins, and fats. It takes these nutrients to all your cells, so that they can keep working and growing.

How Blood Circulates

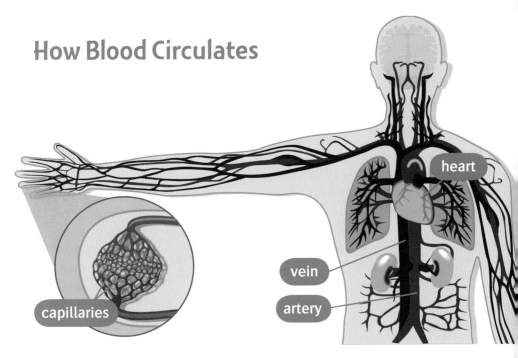

Your blood moves, or circulates, around your body through special tubes called arteries, capillaries, and veins. Arteries take blood away from the heart and they divide into smaller tubes called capillaries. The capillaries take the blood to all the cells of the body.

From the cells, the blood flows into veins and goes back to the heart. When the blood gets back to the heart, it's dark red because it doesn't have very much oxygen left. To get more oxygen, the blood is pumped back to the lungs. When that happens, the blood changes to a bright red color.

Discover!

People can donate blood at the hospital. Doctors use the blood to help people who are sick and need operations.

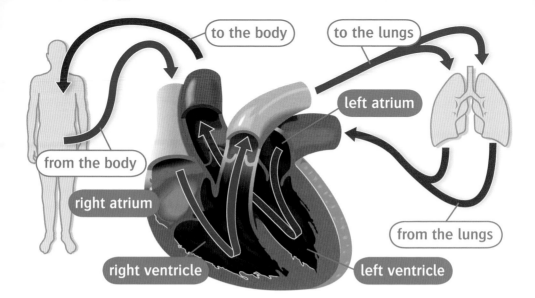

to the body

to the lungs

left atrium

from the body

right atrium

from the lungs

right ventricle

left ventricle

How Your Heart Works

Your heart is a muscle that is divided into four parts
– the right atrium, the right ventricle, the left atrium,
and the left ventricle. Together they make an amazing
natural pump. The right atrium takes blood from all
the parts of your body and sends it to the right
ventricle. Then the right ventricle pumps the blood to
your lungs, where it gets oxygen. After it gets oxygen,
the blood returns to your heart. It goes into the left
atrium and then into the left ventricle. Then the left
ventricle pumps the blood all around your body.

Discover!

The left side of the heart is
bigger than the right side. That's
because the left ventricle has to
pump blood all around your body.

Cleaning Your Blood

Your blood takes waste from your cells and transports it to your kidneys. Then your kidneys take the waste and mix it with water. This makes a liquid called urine. The urine goes to your bladder, and then it leaves your body when you go to the toilet. Remember to drink lots of water every day. Your kidneys need water to keep your blood clean!

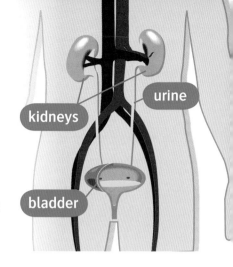

kidneys

urine

bladder

Some people's kidneys don't work well, so they need help to clean their blood. Doctors can use a dialysis machine to clean their blood for them. Sometimes, doctors can also transplant a kidney that is donated by another person.

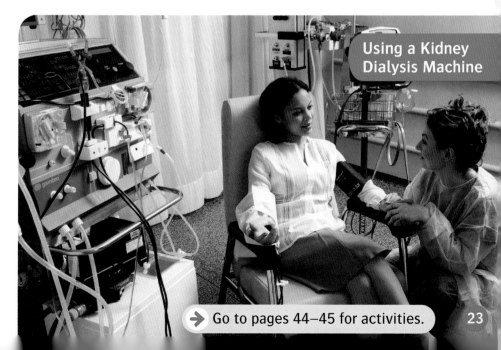

Using a Kidney Dialysis Machine

→ Go to pages 44–45 for activities.

6 Food and Digestion

Do you know what happens to your food after you eat it? Your body gets nutrients from your food, like proteins, carbohydrates, and fats. This is called digestion. Do you know how it happens?

Healthy Food

The food that you eat has important nutrients. Meat, fish, and eggs give you proteins for healthy muscles. Other food, like bread, rice, and pasta, gives you carbohydrates for energy. Fruit and vegetables are very important, too. They give you vitamins and minerals that you need to stay healthy. Your body also needs fats to grow and to keep warm. You can get healthy fats from food like fish, milk, and nuts.

Digestion

Digestion starts in your mouth. First you use your teeth to bite and chew your food. You also use your tongue to move the food around in your mouth. Your mouth produces a liquid called saliva. It makes food softer, so that you can chew and swallow easily.

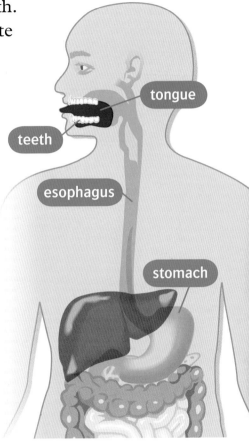

When you swallow, the food goes into a long tube called the esophagus. The esophagus takes the food down to your stomach. Then your stomach mixes the food with gastric juices, and they change the food into a wet paste. Your body can digest this more easily.

Discover!

Don't have too many sweet foods or sugary drinks. They can make you fat and they aren't good for your teeth!

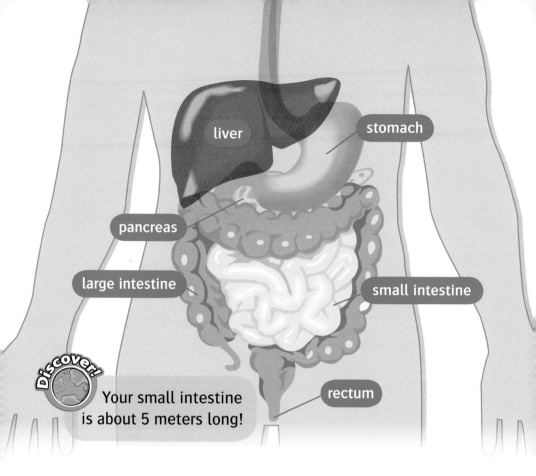

liver

stomach

pancreas

large intestine

small intestine

Discover!

Your small intestine is about 5 meters long!

rectum

From your stomach, the wet paste goes into a long tube called the small intestine. This is where your body breaks down most of the food and takes in most of the nutrients. The nutrients go through the walls of your small intestine and into your blood. Then the rest of the wet paste goes into your large intestine.

The paste that goes into the large intestine isn't food any more. It's solid waste and water. The large intestine takes away most of the water, and then the rest of the waste goes to the rectum. The waste finally leaves your body when you go to the toilet.

Sugar and Insulin

When you eat carbohydrates, your body breaks them down into sugar. Then the sugar goes into your blood. Your cells use some of the sugar for energy. The extra sugar goes to your liver, where it is stored for later.

Your pancreas is under your stomach and it makes a special chemical called insulin. Insulin lets your cells take sugar from your blood. Then your cells can use the sugar for energy.

Some people have diabetes. Their pancreas doesn't make enough insulin, or sometimes it can't make any insulin. Then they can have too much sugar in their blood. People with diabetes have to be careful about what they eat, and sometimes they have to check how much sugar is in their blood. Some people also need insulin injections to control the amount of sugar in their blood.

Checking Blood Sugar

➜ Go to pages 46–47 for activities.

Your brain and nerves are made of nerve cells. Your brain controls everything that happens in your body. It sends and receives messages all the time. These messages are tiny electrical signals that travel through your nerves.

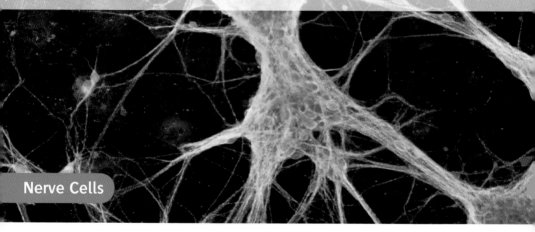

Nerve Cells

How Nerve Cells Work

Nerve cells are a long, irregular shape. At one end they have many branches called dendrites. At the other end, they have a long tail called an axon. The dendrites receive tiny electrical signals from other nerve cells around them. Then the signals travel down the axon and go to other nerve cells.

Discover!

Your brain contains about 100 billion nerve cells.

Your Brain

Your brain has different parts that control different things. The largest part of your brain is the cerebrum. This is where you do most of your thinking. The cerebrum is also where you remember things that happen to you. The cerebellum is at the back of your brain. It helps to control your muscles. Your cerebellum also helps you to keep your balance, so you don't fall down and hurt yourself!

The brain stem controls the most important parts of your body, like your lungs and heart. It does these things automatically, so you don't have to think about them. The brain stem also joins your brain to your spinal cord and the rest of your body.

The Parts of the Brain

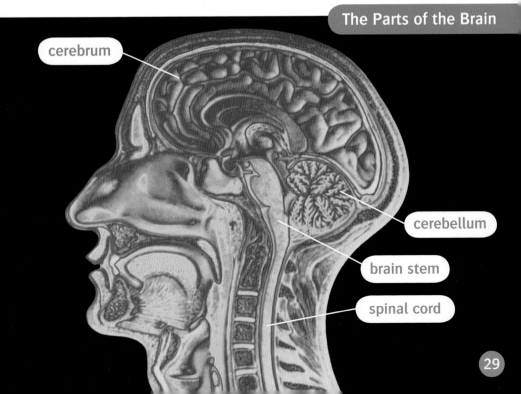

cerebrum

cerebellum

brain stem

spinal cord

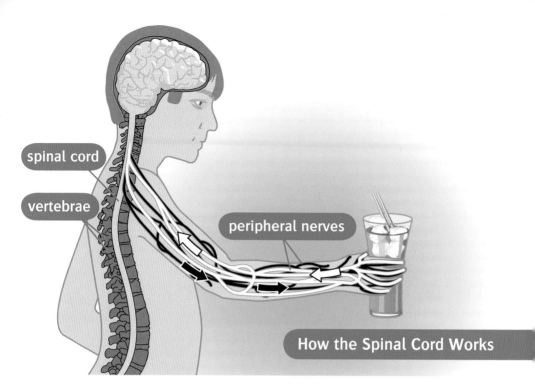

spinal cord

vertebrae

peripheral nerves

How the Spinal Cord Works

Your Spinal Cord

Your spinal cord contains many nerves. They let your brain communicate with the rest of your body. These nerves are very important, so your spinal cord is protected by bones called vertebrae. These are the bones that form your neck and backbone.

Your peripheral nerves join the different parts of your body to your spinal cord and your brain. Some peripheral nerves take information to your brain. For example, the nerves in your fingers give your brain information about the things that you touch. Other peripheral nerves take messages in the other direction. They let your brain control your muscles and all the other parts of your body.

Nervous Diseases

Some diseases, like multiple sclerosis or Alzheimer's disease, can damage nerve cells. There are medicines that help people with these diseases, and doctors are trying to find new cures.

Multiple sclerosis damages nerve cells in the brain and the rest of the body. The damaged cells can't send signals well, so people with multiple sclerosis can have problems controlling their muscles. Sometimes, they can't walk and they need to use a wheelchair.

Alzheimer's disease damages nerve cells in the brain. People with this disease often get confused or forget things. Some people forget where they are, and other people forget their family and friends. Alzheimer's disease is more common in older people, but younger adults can have it, too.

Helping a Person with Multiple Sclerosis

Go to pages 48–49 for activities.

8 Your Body's Defenses

How does your body heal broken bones or cuts? How does it fight infections? What can you do to help your body to defend itself and stay healthy? Read and discover the answers!

Healing Broken Bones

Your bones are very strong, but they can break if you have an accident. When this happens, you should go to hospital. The doctors can use an X-ray machine to see where the bone is broken. Then they can put it back into the right place.

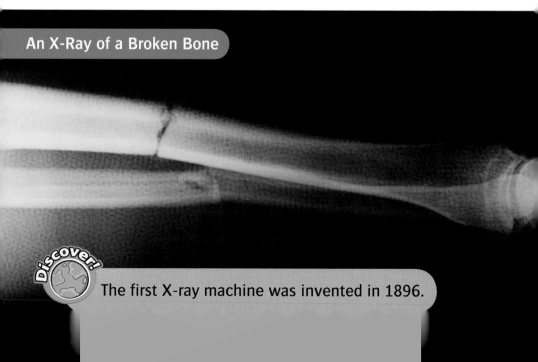

An X-Ray of a Broken Bone

Discover!
The first X-ray machine was invented in 1896.

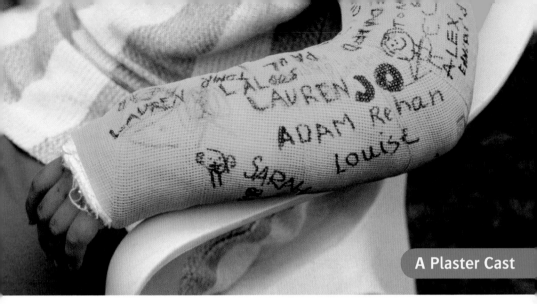

A Plaster Cast

Sometimes you need to wear a plaster cast to help a broken bone to heal. A plaster cast holds the broken parts of the bone together and helps to keep them straight. Then your body starts to grow new bone cells to join the broken parts.

Healing Cuts

If you cut yourself by accident, the cut can bleed a lot at first, but then the bleeding stops. This happens because your body closes the capillaries around the cut. Your blood also has lots of special cells, called platelets. They stick together to make a clot that stops the flow of blood.

After a cut stops bleeding, the dry clot forms a scab. The scab is hard, and it protects the cut from germs. Then new skin cells start to grow under the scab. When the cut is healed, the scab falls off and you can see the new skin. It looks smooth and pink.

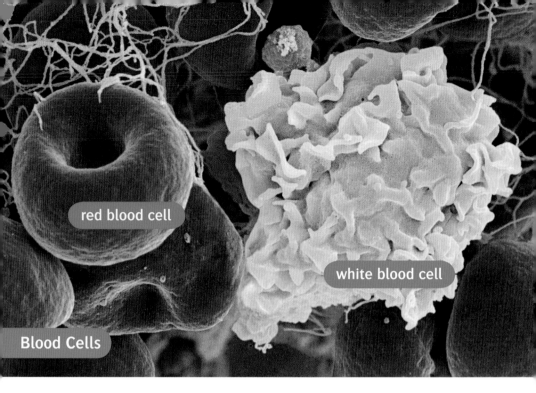

red blood cell

white blood cell

Blood Cells

Fighting Infections

When you hurt yourself, some germs can get into your body through cuts in your skin. There are also germs in the air that we breathe, the food that we eat, and the things that we touch. To defend itself, your body produces white blood cells. They kill the germs and keep your body healthy.

Sometimes you can get a fever when you have an infection. Your body temperature increases, and you start to sweat to help your body to cool down. This is another way that your body tries to fight infection. Your body increases its temperature to kill the germs, but a high fever can be dangerous. When you have a high fever, you should see a doctor.

Help Your Body!

You can help your body to defend itself and stay healthy. Give your body the nutrients that it needs. Eat a variety of healthy foods and drink lots of water.

Do exercise to keep your heart, lungs, muscles, and bones strong. Protect your lungs – don't smoke!

Get enough sleep every night so your body can rest. Your body heals itself when you are sleeping.

Keep your body clean. Take baths or showers regularly, and wash your hands before you eat. Don't forget to brush your teeth, too!

Protect your body from danger. Use safety equipment when you do sport, and always wear a seat belt when you ride in a car. It can save your life! Your body is amazing. Remember to care for it!

→ Go to pages 50–51 for activities.

1 Cells and Growth

← Read pages 4–7.

1 Complete the sentences.

membrane   things   ~~cells~~   cytoplasm   nucleus

1 Your ___cells___ are the smallest living parts of your body.

2 Some living _____ have only one cell.

3 The _____ is the jelly inside a cell.

4 The _____ protects a cell.

5 The _____ controls everything inside a cell.

2 Correct the sentences.

1 A human body has about a billion cells.

   A human body has more than ten trillion cells.

2 A cell's nucleus is outside the membrane.

   _____

3 Water can't go through the cell membrane.

   _____

4 Red blood cells are an irregular shape.

   _____

5 Your muscle cells are short and thin.

   _____

3 Complete the sentences. Then number them in order.

embryo   nine months   egg cell   fetus   sperm cell

[ ] The embryo gets bigger and it's called a _____ .

[ ] The baby is finally born after about _____ .

[1] The mother produces an _____ .

[ ] The new cell divides many times to form an _____ .

[ ] The egg cell joins with the father's _____ .

4 Answer the questions.

1 How much do most babies weigh on their first birthday?

They weigh about three times more than when
they were born.

2 When do most children learn to talk?

_____

3 When do children become adolescents?

_____

4 When do most people stop getting taller?

_____

5 What happens to adults' skin when they get older?

_____

6 What do many older people do?

_____

2 Skin, Hair, and Nails

← Read pages 8–11.

dermis   ~~epidermis~~   fat cells
hair follicle   oil gland
pore   sweat gland   hair

1 Write the words.

1 _epidermis_
2 _____
3 _____
4 _____
5 _____
6 _____
7 _____
8 _____

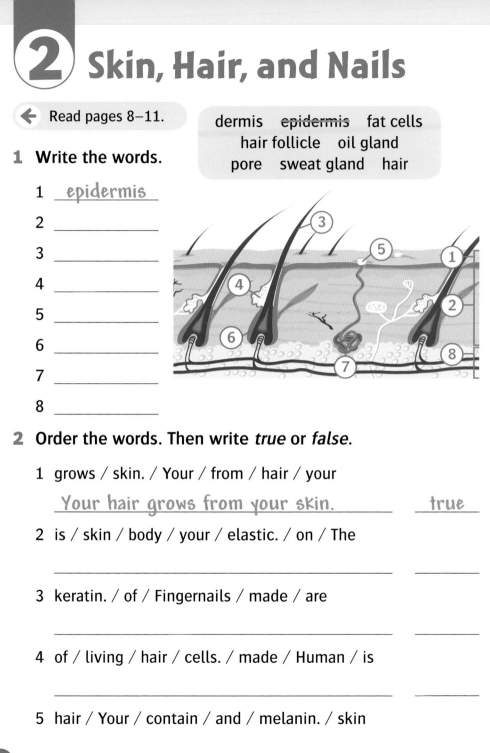

2 Order the words. Then write _true_ or _false_.

1 grows / skin. / Your / from / hair / your

Your hair grows from your skin.   _true_

2 is / skin / body / your / elastic. / on / The

_____   _____

3 keratin. / of / Fingernails / made / are

_____   _____

4 of / living / hair / cells. / made / Human / is

_____   _____

5 hair / Your / contain / and / melanin. / skin

_____   _____

3 **Complete the sentences.**

head   melanin   toenails   oil   pores   root

1 Your dermis has glands that produce _____ .

2 Dark hair contains more _____ than fair hair.

3 Your _____ protect the soft ends of your toes.

4 Sweat leaves your body through tiny _____ .

5 Each fingernail grows from a _____ .

6 The skin on your _____ loses a lot of heat.

4 **Answer the questions.**

1 Why do older people get wrinkles in their skin?

_____

2 When does the hair on your body stand up?

_____

3 How much do your fingernails grow every month?

_____

4 How much do your toenails grow every month?

_____

5 What happens when sweat dries on your skin?

_____

6 How many hairs do you lose every day?

_____

3 Bones and Muscles

← Read pages 12–15.

1 Write the words.

arm   femur
hand   hip   foot
knee   rib   skull

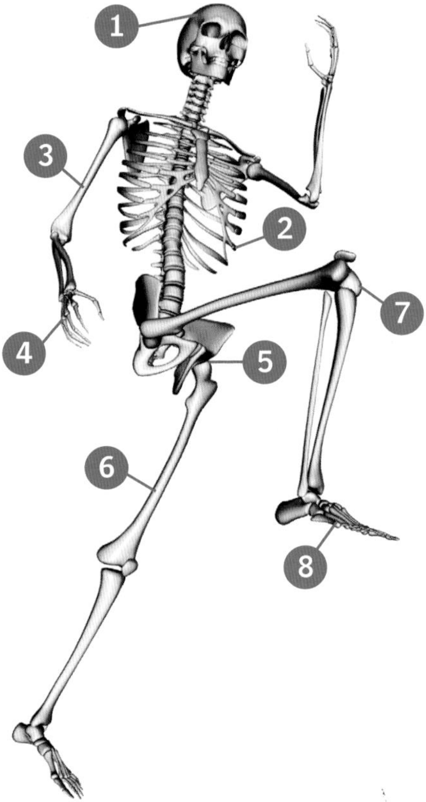

1 _____

2 _____

3 _____

4 _____

5 _____

6 _____

7 _____

8 _____

2 Circle the correct words.

1 You have 26 bones in each of your **hands** / **feet**.

2 Your biceps are muscles in your **legs** / **arms**.

3 Your **hip** / **knee** joint can move in many ways.

4 Some of your **muscles** / **bones** have spaces inside.

5 Muscles get **longer** / **shorter** when they contract.

3 **Match. Then write the sentences.**

Your ossicles are the	between the bones in your joints.
The marrow is where	your muscles to your bones.
You have cartilage	smallest bones in your body.
Your tendons join	do their work automatically.
Involuntary muscles	your body grows new red blood cells.

1 *Your ossicles are the smallest bones in your body.*

2 _____

3 _____

4 _____

5 _____

4 **Answer the questions.**

1 Why do you have cartilage in your joints?

_____

2 What's the biggest bone in the human body?

_____

3 How many times does your heart beat every day?

_____

4 What part of your body does your skull protect?

_____

5 What important nutrient can we get from meat?

_____

4 Lungs and Breathing

← Read pages 16–19.

1 Write the words.

alveoli   bronchi
air   bronchioles
lung   trachea

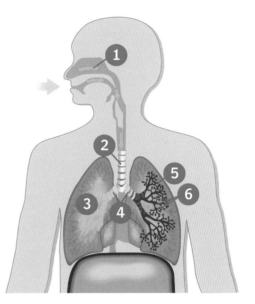

1 _____

2 _____

3 _____

4 _____

5 _____

6 _____

2 Complete the sentences.

asthma   lungs   oxygen
red blood cells   tanks   waste gas

1 Your body takes _____ from the air that you breathe.

2 Carbon dioxide is a _____ that your cells produce.

3 Your _____ take oxygen around your body.

4 Some divers use air _____ to breathe underwater.

5 People with _____ can have problems breathing.

6 Smoking makes people's _____ very dirty.

3 Complete the chart.

air tank   high altitudes   mouthpiece
mask   oxygen tank   underwater

Diver	Mountain Climber
air tank	

4 Write *true* or *false*.

1 There is more oxygen at high altitudes. _____

2 Your capillaries have very thin walls. _____

3 Living things don't need oxygen. _____

4 You breathe out carbon dioxide. _____

5 Fish take oxygen from water. _____

5 Answer the questions.

1 How many alveoli do you have in each lung?

_____

2 How can people with asthma take their medicine?

_____

3 How many people does smoking kill every year?

_____

4 How long can most people hold their breath?

_____

5 Blood and Circulation

← Read pages 20–23.

1 Circle the correct words.

1 Your **white** / **red** blood cells transport oxygen.

2 Your capillaries are **bigger** / **smaller** than your arteries.

3 Your **veins** / **kidneys** clean your blood and make urine.

4 Your veins take blood **back to** / **away from** your heart.

5 Your kidneys need **water** / **waste** to work properly.

2 Complete the sentences. Then number them in order.

left atrium   left ventricle
to the lungs   right atrium
right ventricle
to the whole body

☐ The right ventricle pumps blood _____.

☐ The _____ gets blood from the whole body.

☐ The left ventricle pumps blood _____.

☐ The right atrium sends blood to the _____.

☐ The left atrium sends blood to the _____.

☐ From the lungs, the blood goes to the _____.

3 Complete the diagram.

carbon dioxide   fats   oxygen   proteins
red blood cells   sugar   white blood cells

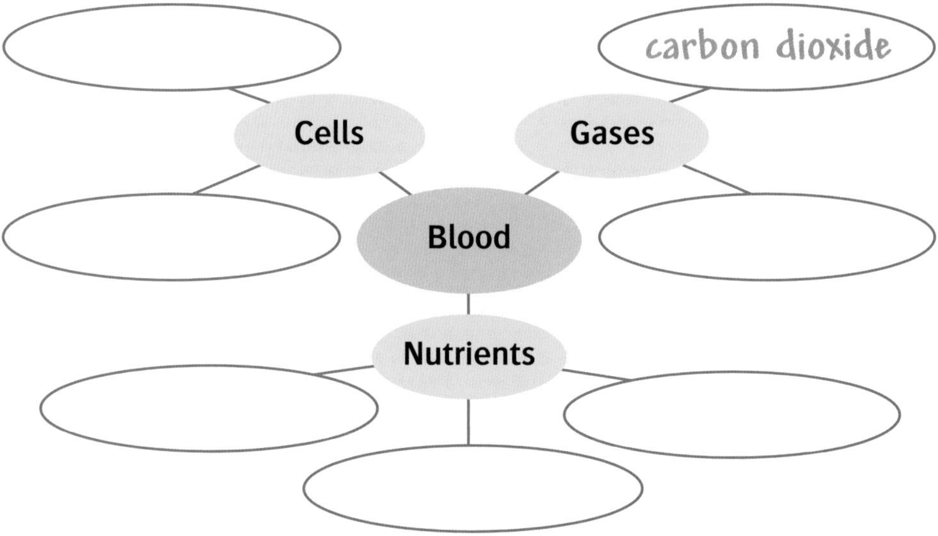

(_____)

carbon dioxide

Cells

Gases

(_____)

Blood

(_____)

Nutrients

(_____)

(_____)

(_____)

4 Answer the questions.

1 When does your blood change to a bright red color?

_____

2 How many red blood cells does your body have?

_____

3 What does a dialysis machine do?

_____

4 Which side of your heart is bigger?

_____

5 Why do people donate blood at the hospital?

_____

6 Food and Digestion

← Read pages 24–27.

1 Write the words.

large intestine   esophagus
pancreas   rectum
small intestine   stomach

1 _____

2 _____

3 _____

4 _____

5 _____

6 _____

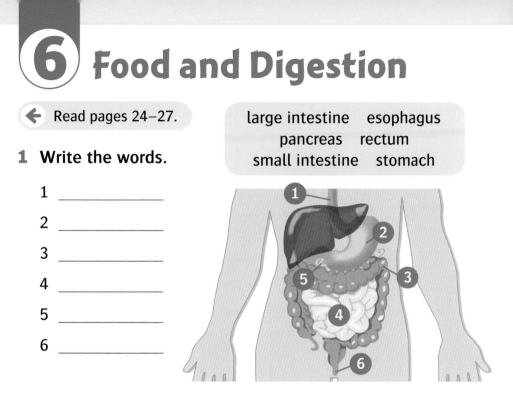

2 Match. Then write the sentences.

Your body gets nutrients	move food around in your mouth.
You use your teeth	easier to chew and swallow.
Your tongue helps to	from your food.
Saliva makes food	the food with gastric juices.
Your stomach mixes	to bite and chew your food.

1 _____

2 _____

3 _____

4 _____

5 _____

3 **Order the words. Then write *true* or *false*.**

1 and / carbohydrates. / Meat / you / fish / give

_____   _____

2 for / body / Your / energy. / vitamins / uses

_____   _____

3 long. / about / small intestine / Your / 2 meters / is

_____   _____

4 to grow. / fats / body / doesn't / any / need / Your

_____   _____

5 produces / Your / insulin. / chemical / pancreas / called / a

_____   _____

4 **Answer the questions.**

1 Why do you need to eat fruit and vegetables?

_____

2 What does your large intestine do?

_____

3 Why do some people with diabetes need insulin injections?

_____

4 What happens to nutrients in your small intestine?

_____

5 What takes food from your mouth to your stomach?

_____

7 The Brain and Nerves

← Read pages 28–31.

1 Complete the puzzle. Then write the secret word.

1 Your vertebrae are bones that __ your spinal cord.
2 The brain __ everything that happens in the body.
3 Your cerebrum is where you __ things that happen to you.
4 Diseases like multiple sclerosis can __ nerve cells.
5 Your brain __ and receives messages through your nerves.
6 The brain stem __ your brain to your spinal cord.
7 Dendrites are the parts of a nerve cell that __ signals.
8 Your brain __ about 100 billion nerve cells.
9 Some peripheral nerves __ information to the brain.
10 Your cerebellum helps you to __ your balance.

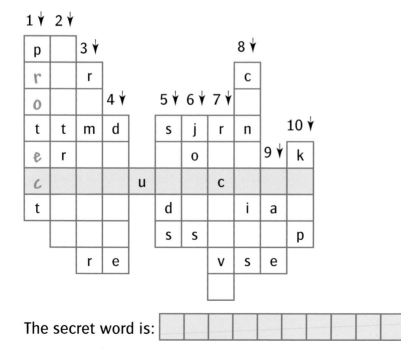

The secret word is: ⬚⬚⬚⬚⬚⬚⬚⬚⬚⬚⬚⬚⬚

2 Write the words.

brain stem
cerebellum
cerebrum
spinal cord
vertebrae

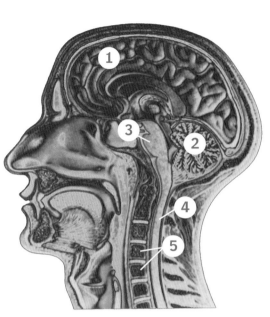

1 _____

2 _____

3 _____

4 _____

5 _____

3 Answer the questions.

1 What is the long tail of a nerve cell called?

_____

2 What part of your brain controls your heart?

_____

3 Why do people with Alzheimer's disease forget things?

_____

4 What bones form your neck and backbone?

_____

5 What shape are your nerve cells?

_____

8 Your Body's Defenses

← Read pages 32–35.

1 Complete the sentences.

> high fever   plaster cast   platelets
> scab   sleep   white blood cells

1 Your _____ are cells that help to stop bleeding.

2 A _____ forms to protect a cut from germs.

3 Your _____ kill germs that get into your body.

4 A _____ helps to keep broken bones straight.

5 When you have a _____ , you should see a doctor.

6 You need to get enough _____ every night.

2 Correct the sentences.

1 New skin cells grow on top of a scab.

_____

2 There are no germs in the air that we breathe.

_____

3 A plaster cast keeps broken bones smooth.

_____

4 When you sweat you help your body to warm up.

_____

5 Your body can grow new bone clots.

_____

3 Write the words.

1 rkebno   <u>broken</u>   5 ljalscaprie   <u>c   </u>

2 nectnifio   <u>i   </u>   6 raetrempetu   <u>t   </u>

3 pmenqeuit   <u>e   </u>   7 gasdnerou   <u>d   </u>

4 idetcacn   <u>a   </u>   8 lgbedein   <u>b   </u>

4 Answer the questions.

1 What happens to the capillaries around a cut?

_____

2 When does a scab finally fall off?

_____

3 Why do doctors use X-ray machines?

_____

4 How long ago was the X-ray machine invented?

_____

5 How do white blood cells fight infections?

_____

5 How can you help your body to defend itself and to stay healthy?

_____

_____

_____

_____

_____

A Body Quiz

1 Write more true or false sentences about the human body.

Do the Body Quiz!

Write _true_ or _false_.

1 Your body has more than ten trillion cells. _____
2 Your hair isn't made of living cells. _____
3 _____ _____
4 _____ _____
5 _____ _____
6 _____ _____
7 _____ _____
8 _____ _____
9 _____ _____
10 _____ _____
11 _____ _____
12 _____ _____

2 Give your quiz to friends or people in your family.

3 Display your quiz and the results.

A Body Poster

1 Choose one part of the body, for example, the skin.

2 Write notes.

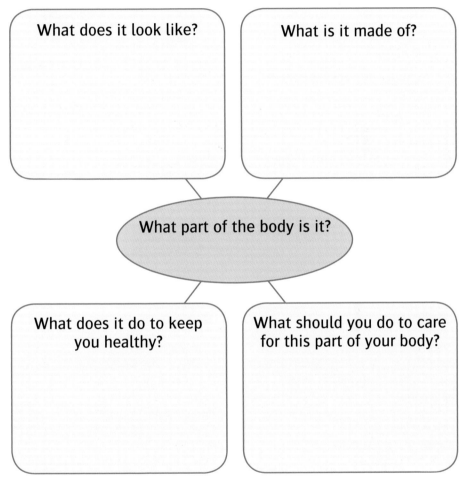

What does it look like?

What is it made of?

What part of the body is it?

What does it do to keep you healthy?

What should you do to care for this part of your body?

3 Make a poster about this part of the body. Write sentences and add pictures or photos.

4 Display your poster.

Glossary

accident something that happens by chance

adolescence the time in life when someone is between about 11 and 15 years old

adult a man or a woman; not a child

adulthood the time in life when someone is an adult

altitude how high a place is

beans the seeds of a plant that we eat

beat to make a regular movement (for the heart)

become to change into; to start to be

bend to make something not straight; to become not straight

bite to use your teeth to cut through something

bleed to lose blood

blood the red liquid in your body

brain the part of a body inside the head; it controls everything that happens in the body

branch (*plural* **branches**) a part of a tree that grows out from the main part

break down to divide something into smaller parts

breathe to take in and let out air through your nose and mouth

bright strong and easy to see (for colors)

cancer a very dangerous disease

carbohydrate a nutrient that the body can change into sugar and use for energy

center the middle

change to become different

check to find out something

chemical a solid or liquid that is made by chemistry

chest the top part of the front of the body

chew to bite food into smaller pieces

childhood the time in life when someone is a child

common usual; seen in many places

communicate to give and receive information

contain to have something inside

continue to keep doing something

contract to become smaller or shorter (for muscles)

control to make something work the way that you want

cover to be over something

cure something that makes someone healthy again

dairy product foods made from milk

damage to make something bad or weak

dead not living any more

defend to keep something safe

disease a medical problem that makes you sick

divide to break into smaller parts

donate to give something that helps other people

elastic when you pull something elastic, it goes back to its original shape

electrical related to electricity

energy we need energy to move and grow

enough how much we want or need

esophagus (*or* **oesophagus**) the long tube that takes food from your mouth to your stomach

exercise what we do when we move to stay healthy

extra more than usual

fair not dark (for hair)

fiber something that looks like a thin string

flexible can move easily

flow to move from one place to another (for liquids)

form to make or be made

gas not a solid or liquid; like air

gastric juice a liquid in the stomach that helps to digest food

germ a small living thing that causes disease

gland a part of the body that makes special chemicals

grow to get bigger

heal to make something healthy

healthy not sick; good for you

heart the part of the body that moves blood around the body

hole a space in something

hurt when something is sore or causes pain

increase to get bigger; to make something bigger

independent able to do things without help

infection a health problem that is caused by germs

information what you know about something

irregular not regular

irritated sore and often red

jelly a thick liquid

keep to stay or make something stay the same

kill to make something or someone die

layer a flat section of something, like the top of your skin

liquid not solid or gas

lung one of two parts of the body in the chest that you use for breathing

medicine something that you take when you are sick, to make you better

muscle a part of the body that you contract or relax to move bones

natural something that comes from nature; it's not made by people

nutrient something that your body needs like food, water, and oxygen

oil a fatty liquid

operation doctors do this when they cut open part of the body to repair it

oxygen a gas that we need to breathe

pair two things the same

paste a soft, wet mixture

platelets cells in the blood that make it stop flowing

produce to grow or to make something

protect to keep safe from danger

protein a nutrient that the body uses to grow things like muscles or nails

pump to push liquid through a tube

receive to get something

regular often doing the same thing; having the same shape

relax to stop contracting (for muscles)

replace to change one thing for another

reproduce to make a copy

rest to do little or nothing after working

root the part that joins something to the rest of the body (for nails, hair, teeth)

safety equipment the things that you use to keep safe

seat belt the safety belt that you wear in a car, bus, or plane

shape for example, circle, square, triangle

signal a piece of information

solid hard; not liquid or gas

special different and important

store to keep something to use later

support to hold something up

surface the outside or the top of something

swallow to make food move from the mouth into the esophagus

sweat liquid that comes out of our skin when we get very hot

temperature how hot or cold something is

tiny very small

transplant when doctors take a part of the body from one person and put it into another person

transport to take something from one place to another

trillion 1,000,000,000,000

tube a long, thin container that is open at both ends

variety a mixture of different things

waste to use something more than you have to; things that we throw away

waterproof can keep water out

weigh to find out how heavy something is

wheelchair a special chair used by people who can't walk very well

wrinkle a small line in the skin

Oxford Read and Discover

Series Editor: Hazel Geatches • CLIL Adviser: John Clegg

Oxford Read and Discover graded readers are at six levels, for students from age 6 and older. They cover many topics within three subject areas, and support English across the curriculum, or Content and Language Integrated Learning (CLIL).

Available for each reader:
• Audio Pack
• Activity Book

Available for selected readers:
• e-Books

Teaching notes & CLIL guidance: **www.oup.com/elt/teacher/readanddiscover**

Subject Area / Level	The World of Science & Technology	The Natural World	The World of Arts & Social Studies
1 300 headwords	• Eyes • Fruit • Trees • Wheels	• At the Beach • In the Sky • Wild Cats • Young Animals	• Art • Schools
2 450 headwords	• Electricity • Plastic • Sunny and Rainy • Your Body	• Camouflage • Earth • Farms • In the Mountains	• Cities • Jobs
3 600 headwords	• How We Make Products • Sound and Music • Super Structures • Your Five Senses	• Amazing Minibeasts • Animals in the Air • Life in Rainforests • Wonderful Water	• Festivals Around the World • Free Time Around the World
4 750 headwords	• All About Plants • How to Stay Healthy • Machines Then and Now • Why We Recycle	• All About Desert Life • All About Ocean Life • Animals at Night • Incredible Earth	• Animals in Art • Wonders of the Past
5 900 headwords	• Materials to Products • Medicine Then and Now • Transportation Then and Now • Wild Weather	• All About Islands • Animal Life Cycles • Exploring Our World • Great Migrations	• Homes Around the World • Our World in Art
6 1,050 headwords	• Cells and Microbes • Clothes Then and Now • Incredible Energy • Your Amazing Body	• All About Space • Caring for Our Planet • Earth Then and Now • Wonderful Ecosystems	• Food Around the World • Helping Around the World